This book belongs to

who made their first Penance on

in this Church

a gift from

Jesus Speaks to me About Confession

by Angela M. Burrin

illustrated by Maria Cristina Lo Cascio

Come Meet Me in Confession
Matthew 19:13-15

I am Jesus, and I'm so pleased that you are reading this book. Have you made your first Confession yet? If you haven't, I hope you are looking forward to it! Confession is also called the Sacrament of Reconciliation. It is my invitation to you to receive forgiveness of your sins.

When you go to Confession, you meet me there. You won't see me, but you will see the priest. In Confession, he takes my place. He received this special privilege when he was ordained. He won't tell your sins to anyone. All priests make a promise not to repeat what they hear in Confession.

It makes me so happy when I see your parents or teachers bringing you to Confession. It reminds me of the day when some moms and dads brought their children to me to receive a blessing. My disciples thought I was too busy. But I am never too busy to bless children. I said, "Let the little children come to me."

In Confession I give you special graces to help you keep these two great commandments: love your heavenly Father and love one another. I have a lot more to tell you about Confession, so please turn the page and keep reading!

Jesus, I'm so happy that I can meet you in Confession!

Who Committed the First Sin?
Genesis 3

Do you know why you go to Confession? It's because sin entered the world. When my Father created the first man and woman, Adam and Eve, he gave them a beautiful place to live—the Garden of Eden. There was only one very important rule. My Father said, "Because I love you, do not eat the fruit of the tree of the knowledge of good and evil. It will hurt our friendship."

Satan knew about this rule. He tempted Adam and Eve, saying, "If you eat the fruit of the tree of the knowledge of good and evil, you will be like God." Adam and Eve liked what Satan said—it made them feel important. They disobeyed their heavenly Father and chose to eat the forbidden fruit.

Although Adam and Eve had sinned, my Father still loved them. But now they had to leave the Garden of Eden. He placed an angel with a fiery sword to guard the entrance to the garden.

Because of this first sin, called "original sin," everyone is tempted to make wrong choices. Only my mother, Mary, was born without original sin. Ask her to help you avoid the people, places, and things that Satan could use to tempt you.

MARY, MOTHER OF GOD, PRAY FOR ME!

My Father's Amazing Promise
John 19:30

I saw Adam and Eve leave the Garden of Eden. That was a sad day in heaven. But the story didn't end there. My Father made an amazing promise.

The promise was that he would send me—his Son—to earth. I had a very special mission. I told the crowds how much their Father loved them. I healed the sick, changed water into wine, and fed thousands of people with only five loaves and two fishes.

I also did something else. Although I had committed no sin, I suffered and died on a cross for the punishment of sin. I am the Savior of the world. Yes! I have saved you from being punished for your sins. This was my Father's plan for me.

My last words as I hung dying on the cross were "It is finished." At that moment, all sins were forgiven. Satan was defeated. The gates of heaven were opened!

There is more. Three days later, on Easter Sunday, I rose from the dead. Now I am alive, and I am with you all the time! I especially love when you come to Mass and receive me in Holy Communion—and when you meet me in Confession.

JESUS, THANK YOU FOR DYING ON THE CROSS FOR MY SINS.

A Father Who Never Stops Loving You

Luke 15:11-32

Whenever you think about Confession, I want you to remember that my Father is good and kind. There is nothing you can do to make him love you more. And there is nothing you can do that will make him stop loving you.

I wanted the crowds who followed me to know this too. So I told them a parable. A rich man had two sons. The younger son said, "Father, I'm bored. Let me have my share of my inheritance now. I want to leave home and have some fun."

Off he went. He spent all his money doing many wrong things. Then he went to work on a farm. He was so hungry that he wanted to eat the pigs' food. "I'm crazy living like this," he said to himself. "I will go back to my father and say, 'Father, I'm sorry. Let me work here as one of your servants.'"

As he neared his home, his father saw him, ran to him, and hugged him. "Son, I am so happy you are back home with me. I have never stopped loving you!" And he threw a big party to celebrate.

Your Father will always welcome you back too. So during the day, if you do or say something wrong, pray, "Heavenly Father, forgive me."

FATHER, THANK YOU FOR ALWAYS LOVING AND FORGIVING ME.

I Don't Want You to Be a Lost Sheep

Matthew 18:12-14

Here's a parable that shows how much I love you and want to protect you. A shepherd had a hundred sheep. They knew his voice and would come whenever he called them. He led them to graze on good grass and protected them from wolves. One afternoon he said, "It's time to count my sheep . . . ninety-seven, ninety-eight, ninety nine. Oh no! One of my sheep is lost."

The shepherd left the other ninety-nine. He rushed up and down the hillsides, but he couldn't find his lost sheep. Then he heard, "Baa, baa." The bleat became louder. Finally, he saw his sheep down the side of a cliff, caught in some brambles.

The shepherd put his crook around the sheep's neck and gently pulled it to safety. He put it around his shoulders and carried it back to the other ninety-nine. Later, he told everyone, "I have found my lost sheep. I'm so happy!"

I am your Good Shepherd and I am always with you. In Confession I will give you special graces to make good choices so that you can stay close to me—at home, at school, and with your friends.

JESUS, THANK YOU FOR THE GRACE I RECEIVE IN CONFESSION TO STAY CLOSE TO YOU.

The Holy Spirit Will Help You Prepare for Confession

Exodus 20:1-17

How can you prepare to meet me in Confession? Let me tell you! Find a quiet place and ask the Holy Spirit, whom you received at your Baptism, to help you think about what you may have done wrong.

The Holy Spirit might immediately bring some sins to mind. With his help, you can also look over the Ten Commandments and ask yourself: Since my last confession, how well have I loved Jesus? Have I been obedient to my parents and kind to my brothers, sisters, and friends?

The Ten Commandments were given to Moses. Do you remember Moses, who parted the Red Sea so that the Israelites could escape slavery in Egypt? After this, he climbed alone to the top of Mount Sinai. On the mountaintop, my Father wrote the commandments with his finger on two stone tablets. He told Moses, "If the people obey my commandments, I will be their God and they will be my special people."

Try thinking of the Ten Commandments as my Father's love rules! You are one of his special children, and he wants to protect you from doing or saying anything that will hurt you or someone else.

Perhaps you and your family can memorize the Ten Commandments and then quiz each other!

HOLY SPIRIT, THANK YOU FOR REMINDING ME OF MY SINS.

Others Can Help You Prepare for Confession

2 Samuel 12:1-15

As you prepare for Confession, try to remember if your parents, your brothers and sisters, or your teachers have told you that you did something wrong.

This is what happened to David, the king of Israel. One day he saw a beautiful woman named Bathsheba. Although David was married, he thought, "I want that woman to be my wife." So he planned for her husband, Uriah, to be killed in battle. No one knew what David had done. But do you know who did?

David's heavenly Father saw everything that had happened. Because he loved David, my Father wanted him to admit his sin and be forgiven. So he told the prophet Nathan to explain to David what he had done wrong.

Nathan told David this story: "A rich man who had flocks of sheep took the only little lamb of a poor man. He then killed it for a meal for a visitor." David said, "He should be punished." Nathan replied, "You are like that man because you stole another man's wife. You had Uriah killed."

Immediately, David repented of his sins. Later he wrote a beautiful psalm. Perhaps you and your family can read Psalm 51 together.

Heavenly Father, please help me listen to my parents and teachers.

Is There Anyone You Need to Forgive?

Genesis 45:1-8

In the Our Father, you ask my Father to forgive your sins. And he does! You also pray that you will forgive others. When you are thinking about what to confess, you can ask yourself, "Do I need to forgive anyone who has hurt me?"

I know it isn't easy to forgive. I had to forgive two of my disciples: Judas, who betrayed me, and Peter, who said three times that he didn't know me.

Let me tell you a story about forgiveness. A man named Jacob had twelve sons. He loved his son Joseph the best and had given him a beautiful coat of many colors. This made Joseph's brothers jealous. They made plans to hurt him.

One day Jacob sent Joseph to his brothers in the field. His brothers saw him coming and said, "Let's kill him." But instead, they threw him in a well. Then, when travelers from Egypt passed by, his brothers sold him as a slave.

Years later, Joseph was put in charge of all the grain in Egypt. There was a famine, so Joseph's brothers came to Egypt to buy grain. His brothers didn't recognize Joseph, and because he was important, they bowed down to him. Then Joseph said, "I am Joseph! Don't be afraid. I forgive you."

Jesus, please help me to forgive and not hold any grudges against anyone.

It's Time to Confess Your Sins
Luke 23:39-43

Now it's time to go to Confession! When you enter the confessional, the priest will greet you. After you make the Sign of the Cross, say, "Bless me, Father, for I have sinned. It's been (mention how long) since my last Confession."

As you confess your sins, I am listening to you. Remember, in Confession the priest takes my place. He is praying for you. He goes to Confession too, so he knows what it is like. You can tell him anything—even the sins you are embarrassed about. It pleases me when you are honest. And I know that afterwards, you will feel really happy!

Did you know that as I hung high above the crowds on the cross, I heard someone's confession? On either side of me, two criminals were being crucified. One said, "If you are the Christ, why don't you save yourself and us?" The other one, called Dismas, said, "We are being punished for what we have done. But this man has done nothing wrong. Jesus, remember me when you come into your kingdom." I said, "Today, you will be with me in paradise."

After I said that, I'm sure Dismas had a very happy heart! Don't you?

HOLY SPIRIT, PLEASE HELP ME TO ALWAYS MAKE A GOOD CONFESSION.

The Priest Will Give You a Penance

Luke 19:1-10

After you tell the priest your sins, he will give you a penance. It might be a prayer or an act of kindness. When you do your penance, you are showing me that you are sorry for your sins and that you want to try your best not to do the same things again.

Do you know the story of Zacchaeus? One day as I was walking through Jericho, I saw him in a sycamore tree. Because he was short, he had climbed the tree to be able to see me over the crowds. People didn't like Zacchaeus. He was a tax collector and often cheated people. He would make them pay high taxes and keep some of the money for himself.

But I had a special plan for Zacchaeus. So I stopped, looked up at him, and said, "Zacchaeus, I must stay at your house today." He was so happy! Zacchaeus told me, "I will share my money with the poor and I will pay back four times those I have cheated." That was like his penance.

Would you do something for me? If you've hurt someone, tell that person you're sorry. If you've taken anything that wasn't yours, return it. Like Zacchaeus, you can put things right!

JESUS, PLEASE GIVE ME THE COURAGE TO ALWAYS DO WHAT'S RIGHT.

Praying the Act of Contrition
Luke 7:36-50

Now the priest will say, "Make a good Act of Contrition." Pray this special prayer from your heart. My Father is listening. It will make him happy to hear you say that you are sorry for offending him and that you want to try not to sin again.

Once I was invited by Simon the Pharisee to his home for dinner. While I was eating, a woman came and kneeled on the floor beside me. Everyone was shocked because they knew that she had done many wrong things. But I knew that she was sorry for her sins. She was so sorry that she began to cry, and with her tears she washed my feet. Then she kissed my feet, dried them with her long hair, and poured expensive oil on them.

Simon wasn't happy because she was a sinner. I said, "Listen to this story. Two men borrowed money. One borrowed 500 denarii and the other 50 denarii. Later, the lender said to both of them, 'You don't have to pay it back!' Simon, who loved the lender the most?" He answered, "The one who owed the most."

Simon was right. Then I said to the woman, "Your sins are forgiven. Go in peace!"

Father, I am sorry for my sins. I know they hurt our friendship.

Your Sins Are Forgiven!
Mark 2:1-12

Finally, you will receive absolution. The priest will make the Sign of the Cross over you and say, "I absolve you from your sins in the name of the Father, and of the Son, and of the Holy Spirit."

"Absolve" means that your sins are forgiven and forgotten. What a great moment—for you and for me! I'm so happy when your sins are forgiven.

One day four men came with their friend, a paralyzed man, to the house where I was teaching. But because the house was so crowded, they couldn't get inside. Do you know what they did? They went on the roof, made an opening, and lowered the man down on his mat to where I was sitting!

When I saw the faith of his friends, I said to the man, "Your sins are forgiven." This didn't please some of the teachers. But I said, "I have authority on earth to forgive sins." And to the man I said, "Get up! Take up your mat and go home!" He did, and everyone was amazed!

After you say your penance and go home, perhaps you and your family can do something to celebrate. Remember, Confession is my gift to you. I hope to meet you there again soon!

Jesus, please bless the priest who heard my Confession!

A Prayer to the Holy Spirit

Come Holy Spirit,

fill the hearts of your faithful

and kindle in them the fire of your love.

Send forth your Spirit,

and they shall be created.

And you shall renew the face of the earth.

Act of Contrition

My God,

I am sorry for my sins with all my heart.

In choosing to do wrong

and failing to do good,

I have sinned against you

whom I should love above all things.

I firmly intend, with your help,

to do penance,

to sin no more,

and to avoid whatever leads me to sin. Amen.

The Ten Commandments

1. I am the Lord your God: you shall not have strange gods before me.

2. You shall not take the name of the Lord your God in vain.

3. Remember to keep holy the Lord's Day.

4. Honor your Father and Mother.

5. You shall not kill.

6. You shall not commit adultery.

7. You shall not steal.

8. You shall not bear false witness against your neighbor.

9. You shall not covet your neighbor's wife.

10. You shall not covet your neighbor's goods.

Examination of Conscience for Children

Responsibilities to God:

✣ Have I prayed every day?

✣ Have I prayed my morning prayers and night prayers?

✣ Have I prayed with my parents and family?

✣ Have I been moody and rebellious about praying and going to church on Sunday?

✣ Have I asked the Holy Spirit to help me whenever I have been tempted to sin?

✣ Have I asked the Holy Spirit to help me do what is right?

Examination of Conscience for Children

RESPONSIBILITIES TO OTHERS:

✟ Have I been obedient and respectful to my parents?

✟ Have I lied or been deceitful to them or to others?

✟ Have I been arrogant, stubborn, or rebellious?

✟ Have I talked back to parents, teachers, or other adults?

✟ Have I pouted and been moody?

✟ Have I been selfish toward my parents, brothers, and sisters, teachers, or my friends and schoolmates?

✟ Have I gotten angry at them? Have I hit anyone?

✟ Have I held grudges or not forgiven others?

✟ Have I treated other children with respect, or have I made fun of them and called them names?

✟ Have I used bad language?

✟ Have I stolen anything? Have I returned it?

✟ Have I performed my responsibilities, such as homework and household chores?

✟ Have I been helpful and affectionate toward my family?

✟ Have I been kind and generous with my friends?

Psalm 51

God, be merciful to me

Because you are loving.

Because you are always ready to be merciful,

Wipe out all my wrongs.

Wash away all my guilt

And make me clean again.

I know about my wrongs.

I can't forget my sin.

You are the one I have sinned against.

I have done what you say is wrong. . . .

You want me to be completely truthful

So teach me wisdom.

Take away my sin, and I will be clean.

Wash me, and I will be whiter than snow.

Make me hear sounds of joy and gladness.

Create in me a pure heart, God.

Make my spirit right again.

Do not send me away from you.

Do not take your Holy Spirit away from me.

Give me back the joy that comes when you save me.

Keep me strong by giving me a willing spirit.

Then I will teach your ways to those who do wrong.

And sinners will turn back to you. . . .

God, you are the one who saves me.

I will sing about your goodness.

The Jesus Prayer

O Lord Jesus Christ,

Son of God,

have mercy on me,

a sinner.

The Chaplet of Divine Mercy

Eternal Father,

for the sake of His sorrowful passion,

have mercy on us

and on the whole world.

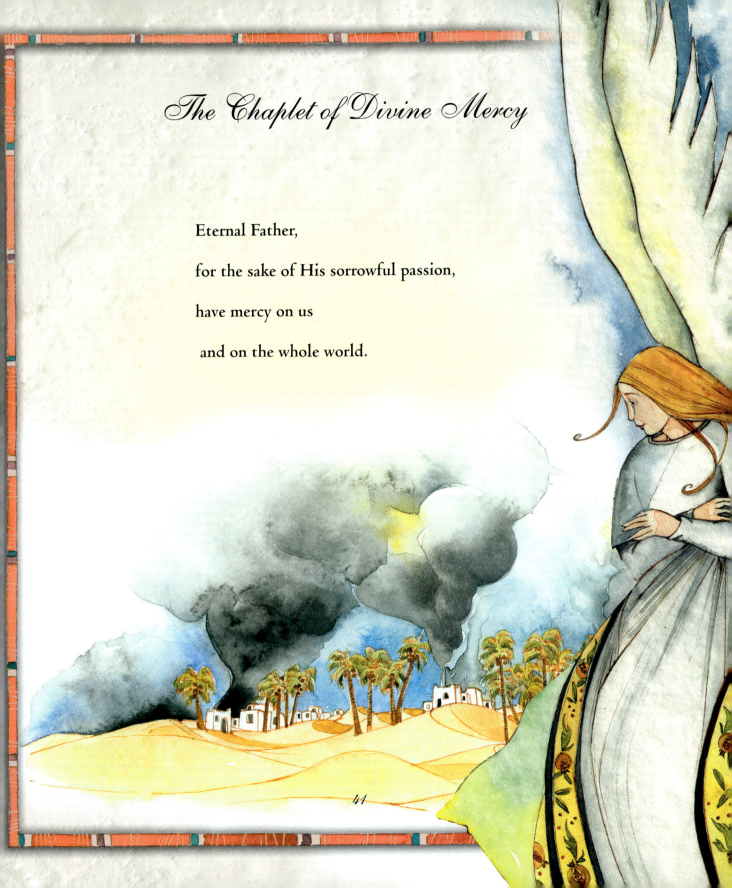

The Our Father

Our Father, who art in heaven,

hallowed be thy name;

thy kingdom come;

thy will be done on earth as it is in heaven.

Give us this day our daily bread;

and forgive us our trespasses

as we forgive those who trespass against us;

and lead us not into temptation

but deliver us from evil. Amen.

The Hail Mary

Hail Mary, full of grace,

the Lord is with you.

Blessed are you among women,

and blessed is the fruit of your womb, Jesus.

Holy Mary, Mother of God,

pray for us sinners,

now and at the hour of our death.

Amen.

Prayer of St. Francis

Lord, make me an instrument of your peace.

Where there is hatred, let me sow love;

Where there is injury, pardon;

Where there is doubt, faith;

Where there is despair, hope;

Where there is darkness, light;

Where there is sadness, joy.

O Divine Master, grant that I may not so much seek

to be consoled as to console;

to be understood as to understand;

to be loved as to love.

For it is in giving that we receive;

it is in pardoning that we are pardoned;

and it is in dying that we are born to eternal life.

Published in 2016 in the U.S. and Canada by
The Word Among Us Press
Frederick, Maryland
www.wau.org

ISBN: 978-1-59325-291-5

Copyright © 2016 Anno Domini Publishing
www.ad-publishing.com
Text copyright © 2016 Angela M. Burrin
Illustrations copyright © 2016 Maria Cristina Lo Cascio

Publishing Director: Annette Reynolds
Art Director: Gerald Rogers
Pre-production: Doug Hewitt

Acknowledgments
Psalm 51 taken from
The Holy Bible, International Children's Bible, 1986, 1988, 1999
by Thomas Nelson, Inc. Used with permission.
Examination of Conscience for Children
was written by Fr. Thomas Weinandy, OFM Cap,
and is reprinted with permission of the author.

Printed and bound in Malaysia
March 2016